A gift to _____

From _____

Della Faye

The Power is within you to
Always Stay Motivated

_____

The Power Is Within You to
Always Stay Motivated

Unless otherwise indicated, all Scripture quotations are taken from the King James Version of the Bible.

The NIV and Message Bible verses are taken from online at www.biblegateway.com

ISBN-13: 978-1936739196
ISBN-10: 1936739194

Cover Design: Sel P.
Publisher: Korloki Publishers, Inc.
Printed in United States of America

CONTENTS

Dedication

This book is dedicated to
my three sons
Terrence Hildreth
Darrell Hildreth
Roy S. Thomas, Jr.

and
my grandchildren

Michael Torres
Kendra Hildreth
Ta'Shai Hildreth
Tiara Hildreth
Terrence, Hildreth Jr. (TJ)
Lela Pennington

INTRODUCTION

The power is within you to Always Stay Motivated

We came into this world with only two fears; the fear of falling and loud noises.

We are instinctively created to grow and excel.

In our infancy we started to sit up, turn over, crawl, and pull ourselves up.

Our curious little minds started touching and feeling things, and even attempting to put things in our mouth; after all, those things were colorful and looked like they were suitable for eating.

We took our first steps; we fell down, but quickly got back up and eventually walked.

We took our first bike ride; we fell off, but quickly got back on and tried again.

Somewhere between our first crawl and first step, as we were growing and discovering things, all of a sudden, we began to *constantly* hear phrases like, *stop, quit, leave that alone, and don't touch.* Sometimes these phrases were yelled to us.

At the time, our parents were keeping us from things which could harm us.

They had our back.

They were protecting us and that was good at the time.

There is one today who has our back, who protects us, that is God.

As human beings, one of our greatest challenges is staying motivated and keeping the faith.

How do you stay motivated and encouraged through the stormy and tragic events that you witness or experience?

How do you cope when your own hopes and dreams are shattered?

Who or what do you turn to?

Do you wallow in sorrow and self-pity?

Do you accept stormy times as necessary events for cleansing, for change, for growth, for happiness, and to bring you closer to God?

Do you believe that tough times are life's lessons—meant to help you grow?

No matter what we've been through, God has the power to raise us up again. Maybe you had children out of wedlock; you may be divorced; you may be living with a sense of failure from drugs or alcohol abuse. It does not matter. God will pick you up and you can come out of any experience and live again if you surrender your life to Him. Just believe, obey, and trust Him.

Another challenge is to keep *stinking thinking* from entering our psyche.

To combat *stinking thinking* requires effort. I encourage you to find and attend motivational events which should include a spiritual service, read motivational books including the most widely read book in the world, the Bible. Surround yourself with optimistic people who will help keep you inspired.

Staying motivated requires more than just drive and ambition. It requires renewing our mind and altering our behavior.

Mr. Zig Ziglar said he was frequently asked the question, *"Why is it that some people get really motivated after listening to you, but after a while slip back into their old, negative ways?"* His response, *"the question really is, is motivation permanent? The answer is no - but then neither is bathing. Motivation is important - not permanent."*

My friend, we make a conscious decision to stay motivated like we make a daily decision to take a bath.

The principles and quotations in this book have educated, encouraged, and led many people through their tough times in life. I encourage you to apply these principles daily.

Thank you to the authors for the encouraging messages in their quotations.

If this book inspires and gives you hope it will have served its purpose. It is a great gift to share with family and friends too.

I wish you love, peace, and joy. God Bless you,

-Della Faye

✟

*"Summing it all up, friends, I'd say you'll do best by filling your minds and meditating on things true, noble, reputable, authentic, compelling, gracious—the best, not the worst; the beautiful, not the ugly; things to praise, not things to curse. Put into practice what you learned from me, what you heard and saw and **realized**. Do that, and God, who makes everything work together, will work you into his most excellent harmonies."*

-*Philippians 4:8* (The Message)

Principle #1
REALIZE—*grasp and understand clearly*

Realize to stay motivated we have to train like an athlete preparing to win the Gold Medal.

Realize we have to act as though today is our last day on the planet and we've been given a chance to fulfill our dreams.

Realize to make the world a better place means we continually have to give our best.

Realize what we do today has a significant impact on our children, and grandchildren.

Realize we are our worst enemy. We must stop sabotaging ourselves. We are the source of the conditions manifested in our life. The one thing we have control over is our thoughts. No one can get into our mind and make us think anything, negative or positive. We choose our thoughts.

The one thing in life we can command is our own mind. Whatever negative situation we face in life, we can always choose a positive attitude.

Realize that negative self-talk will only produce negative results. Make a strong commitment to always choose a positive attitude. Write a LOA, Letter of Agreement to yourself; a meaningful phrase tailored to help you reach your positive thinking goals. Keep it where you can read it several times throughout the day. You can write it on 3 x 5 index cards.

Realize our second enemy—those crabs trying to invade our life. "Crabs" are people who always attempt to pull others down to the bottom of the bucket, instead of piling on top to help people get up over the top and out of the bucket. To stay motivated we must hang around the construction crew not the wrecking crew.

Realize that there are universal (God) laws which are real and true. Laws which we have no control over. Whether we believe it or not. Nothing can come from a human being but another human being. God is magnificent; everything produces after its kind.

Realize we were winners right from the start. We won the very first race we were in. We are *fearfully and wonderfully made. Psalm 139:14.* We were the size of a grain of sand when conceived. Two cells collided, one big and one small. The big cell an egg from the female, the small cell sperm from the male. Millions of them chased the egg, one of them won that race and became one great precious cell—you.

Realize apples will come from apple seeds. Every seed produces after its kind. Negative talk and negative thoughts will produce after their kind too. The person who plants crap will reap weeds.

Hallelujah! I'm glad there are laws that man cannot change--God's laws!

We can change the man-made laws that govern us, like traffic laws and other laws initiated by man. Man can change them because it is man who implemented them. But thank God, man cannot change God's laws.

Realize when stinking thinking is attempting to creep into your mind.

Realize grumbling and complaining leads to wandering in the wilderness. God is listening, and grumbling and complaining will keep us from reaching our Promised Land.

Read the Biblical story of our Lord delivering the children of Israel from their oppressors in Egypt (in the Book of Exodus). He parted the Red Sea right before their eyes, then miraculously provided food and water, led them by a pillar of cloud in the day and pillar of fire at night, and still the people grumbled and complained against the Lord.

As a result of their complaining they were forbidden to enter the Promised Land. Forty years the children of Israel wandered in the wilderness until that ungrateful and complaining generation died. They wandered for forty years on a journey that would have taken only 11 days.

Realize when we need to *watch what we are saying or just shut up.*

Realize God wants us to have faith, not grumble and complain.

Realize grumbling and complaining takes more energy than trust and faith.

Realize to *always stay motivated* we must have faith and remain optimistic. Pessimism leads to uncertainty and a lack of action.

Realize all the good in our lives and stop grumbling. Learn to give thanks in all things.

Realize expressing gratitude and saying thanks accomplishes more. Sing or play the song "*To God Be the Glory,*" to replace *stinking thinking* with thoughts of gratitude and thanksgiving.

✞✞✞✞✞✞

✝

*Seek always to do some good, somewhere. Every man has to seek in his own way to **realize** his true worth. You must give some time to your fellow man. For remember, you don't live in a world all your own. Your brothers are here too.*

-Albert Schweitzer

✞

Sin is like a cancer that destroys step-by-step, sometimes so slowly we don't **realize** *what's happening to us.*

-David Jeremiah

✝

"GOD said to Moses: "Pharaoh is a stubborn man. He refuses to release the people. First thing in the morning, go and meet Pharaoh as he goes down to the river. At the shore of the Nile take the staff that turned into a snake and say to him, 'GOD, the God of the Hebrews, sent me to you with this message: "**Release** my people so that they can worship me in the wilderness." So far you haven't listened. This is how you'll know that I am GOD. I am going to take this staff that I'm holding and strike this Nile River water. The water will turn to blood, the fish in the Nile will die, the Nile will stink, and the Egyptians won't be able to drink the Nile water."

-*Exodus 7:14-18* (The Message)

Principle #2

RELEASE—*set free*

Release old worn out habits that no longer serve you. I grew up in a home with 9 siblings. When we were growing up my parents were very strict about maintaining a clean home. Our dad would wake us from our sleep in the middle of the night, sometimes 2:00 a.m., if a single glass was left in the sink.

His disciplinary actions bothered me and when I became an adult I shared my disappointment with a psychologist.

Her response was "Della, your dad had to establish order because of the number of children being raised." She went on to tell me, "You don't have to continue living by such stringent conditions."

My friend, if you are anything like me, you know that once something is ingrained in you it is like you are on automatic pilot. You become acclimated to that behavior.

After my conversation with the psychologist my behavior changed. I released old worn out habits that no longer served me well.

As a matter of fact, as I look back on my behavior I realized that it probably hindered many of my relationships because of course, I expected "excellence" from everyone, and wouldn't settle for anything less. Why would I not settle for less? My dad didn't and I was mimicking his behavior.

Embrace change when it comes. Wouldn't the world be a boring place if nothing changed? What would the planet look like if people didn't die and everyone continued to live?

God knows what he is doing. It is often said the only constant is change. Therefore don't be afraid to release old habits and issues. God is in control. Everything on earth is being continuously transformed. Realize this principle and you will always stay motivated. **Release** pessimistic thoughts and be *optimistic*—occasionally see the glass half full instead of always seeing it half empty.

Release negative thoughts and fears that hold you back. Address fears ad negative self-talk by consciously speaking to yourself as you would to a very good friend. When the negative thoughts come, say "next;" do not entertain any negative talk.

Release hatred and animosity toward parents, siblings, former spouses, boyfriends/girlfriends or anyone for that matter, who you believe has 'hurt' you.

Release self-sabotaging behaviors.

Release unhealthy self-talk, statements such as I'm not good enough. I'm too skinny. I'm too fat. I'm too short, or I'm too tall. I don't have what it takes. He/she is more educated, all negative thoughts and words.

Release—take a few deep breaths from time-to-time and *just let go*. Set your mind free.

Releasing helps us to free ourselves from negative thoughts.

✚✚✚✚✚✚

✝

*Hatred paralyzes life; love **releases** it.*
Hatred confuses life; love harmonizes it.
Hatred darkens life; love illumines it.

-Martin Luther King, Jr.

****

✝

You leave old habits behind by starting out
*with the thought, "I **release** the need for this in my*
life."

-Dr. Wayne Dyer

✝

Remove impurities from the silver
and the silversmith can craft a fine chalice;
Remove the wicked from leadership
and authority will be credible and God-honoring.

-Proverbs 25:4-5 (The Message)

Principle #3

REMOVE—eliminate, do away with, and get rid of

Remove negative family and friends from your environment.

Remember those crabs I mentioned. You know them. Every person has dealt with a person or two who is an envious or jealous friend, coworker, or family member.

Are any of these people in your household or circle of friends? People who always tell you the reason why something won't work, or why someone is "not the right person for you?" You know those "busy bodies."

Remove yourself from them. You can be cordial, and talk over the telephone. You don't

20

have to break bread with them or allow them to hinder your business and personal affairs. Love and pray for them from a distance if necessary.

And, my friend the same applies to you. Do not be a crab in people's life. If you can't help another person, please don't hinder, pull them down or de-motivate them.

Remove sin from your life. *I Peter 1:15-16* says, *"But as he which hath called you is holy, so be ye holy in all manner of conversation;*

Because it is written, *Be ye holy; for I am holy."*

Remove hatred, anger, animosity, cheating, lying and such.

Remove anything that is a hindrance or barrier to your goals, plans, growth and not pleasing to the Lord.

✝✝✝✝✝✝

✝

*God never promises to **remove** us from our struggles.
He does promise, however, to change the way we look at
them.*

-Max Lucado

****

✝

*Prayer has mighty power to move mountains because the
Holy Spirit is ready both to encourage our praying and to
remove the mountains hindering us.*

-Wesley Duewel

✝

You who are young,
make the most of your youth.
Relish *your youthful vigor.*
Follow the impulses of your heart.
If something looks good to you, pursue it.
But know also that not just anything goes;
You have to answer to God for every last bit of it.
-*Ecclesiastes 11:9* (The Message)

Relish the moments!
As you get older, meditate on your
youthful days, when you laughed, played and enjoyed life.

Pictured: Tiara and Terrence, Jr.

Principle #4

RELISH—*take pleasure in, like, enjoy*

Relish the moment. Too often we put off "living" and taking pleasure in life. We put things off as though we know the day and hour when Christ will return.

Enjoy life now. Take pleasure in your freedom, your right to choose, to go, to plan.

Use the good silverware now. Sit in the family room now. Drive the nice car now. Wear your after five clothes more often. With the money you spent on those clothes, do they adorn the closet more than your body?

Appreciate each moment. Live and enjoy today while it is today. *For one day there will be no tomorrow for one, and many lonely tomorrows for the other.*

Relish each moment with your spouse, friends, children, and other family members. Treasure those moments and make them memorable. Don't tear people down with negativity. Build them up. Say encouraging words.

Take pleasure in people's strengths don't look for their faults and weaknesses. If you do then you won't find time to love and appreciate them. Take pleasure in your own strengths too. Everyone has shortcomings.

✜ ✜ ✜ ✜ ✜ ✜

✝

Relish love in your old age!
Aged love is like aged wine; it becomes more
satisfying, more refreshing, more valuable,
more appreciated and more intoxicating.
-Leo Buscaglia

✝

*As water **reflect**s the face,*
*So one's life **reflect**s the heart.*
-Proverbs 27:19 (NIV)

Principle #5

REFLECT—*think, ponder, and meditate*

Reflect on your *first* achievements in life.

Your *first* day at school

Your *first* savings account (possibly a piggy bank)

Your *first* bicycle (probably a tricycle)

Your *first* car

Your *first* job (even if it was babysitting, stocking for the local grocer, delivering papers)

Your *first* friend

Your *first* date

Your *first* love

Your *first* child

Your *first* _____ (you fill in the blank).

Remember how you felt at each moment. I remember when I was learning to drive. I held the steering wheel tightly as though it was going to fly from my hand. Look at your driving habits now. I bet you can drive with one-hand, something you never thought you could do when you first started driving.

It is amazing how comfortable things become once we overcome our fear. **Reflecting** motivates when you have new challenges and obstacles to overcome. Yes, there is power in **reflecting,** it motivates us into action.

Create a rainy day book. I have a 3-ring binder with all the cards, notes, and nice things people have written to me, and about me. When I feel like having a *pity-party* I pull out the 3-ring binder, sit in a comfortable spot, and read, and reflect on all my accomplishments, the difference I have made in people's life. This is one of the most powerful exercises you can do to bring yourself out of any slump, self-sabotaging, pity-party mood.

Reflect on the positive. Choose to see the lesson God wanted you to learn, in all that you have endured and gone through in life. There truly is light at the end of today's tunnel like there was light at the end of yesterday's tunnel. And, know that tomorrow will bring new challenges and other tunnels too. The Bible said "in life you *will have* trials and tribulations. Be of good cheer."

Reflect - Turn everything off, the TV, radio, computer, and sit in complete silence for 15, 20 or 30 minutes every day. When your thoughts wander to negativity, replace those negative thoughts with a positive thought. *You are in control.* You can't stop the negative from coming *but* you can replace it with the positive. Repeat a single positive word over-and-over again; this will set you free from negative thoughts which produce after their kind.

✞✞✞✞✞✞

✝

And do not be conformed to this world, but be transformed by the **renewing** *of your mind, that you may prove what is that good and acceptable and perfect will of God.*

-*Romans 12:2* (NKJV)

Principle #6

RENEW—revive, make new spiritually, regenerate

Renew your mind by sowing positive seed thoughts. The Bible, *Romans 12:2* says, *Be ye transformed by the renewing of your mind.*

Renew you mind by learning new skills. Learners are leaders!

Renew your mind by attending seminars and workshops.

Renew your mind by reading.

Renew your mind by listening to mentors, gurus, and sometimes even youth. "Out of the mouth of babes. . ."

Renew your mind by meditating, sitting alone in the silence and listening to the Comforter, the Holy Spirit.

Renew your mind with positive thoughts. Be careful what you allow into your mind. The seed thoughts you sow.

Renew your mind—attend a Sunday and mid-week church service.

Renew your mind—engage in relaxing activities, attend retreats, go swimming, riding a bike, other forms of exercise, and vacationing.

✝✝✝✝✝✝

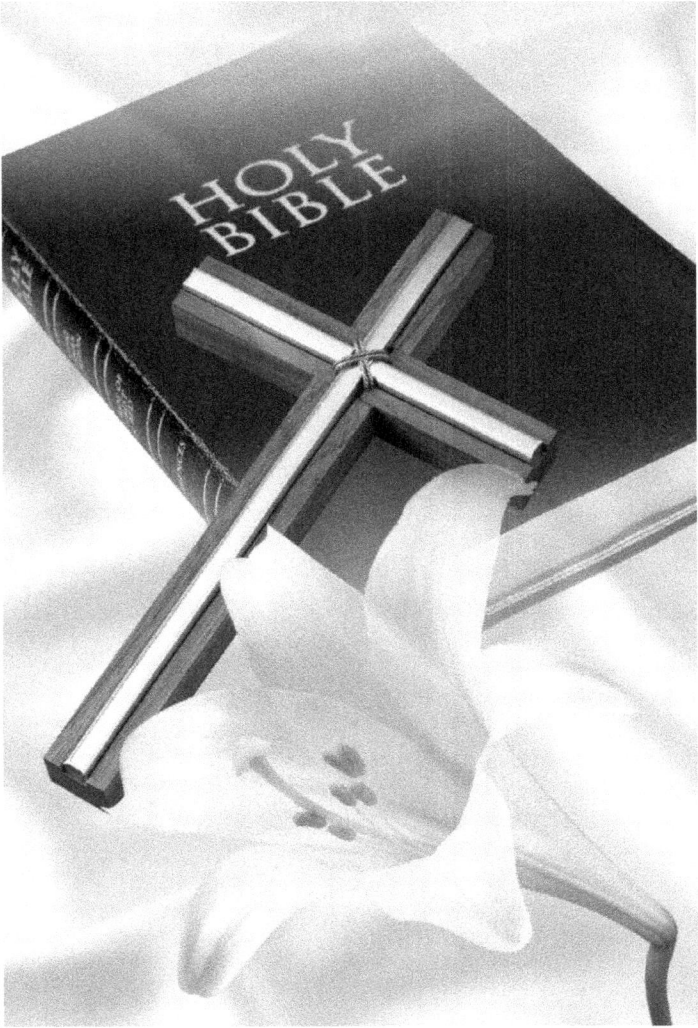

✝

*Moses thought that his own people would realize that God
was using him to rescue them, but they did not.
The next day Moses came upon two Israelites who were
fighting. He tried to **reconcile** them by saying, 'Men you
are brothers; why do you want to hurt each other?'
But the man who was mistreating the other pushed Moses
aside and said, 'Who made you ruler and judge over us?'
-Acts 7:25-27* (NIV)

Principle #7

RECONCILE—*to win over to friendliness; cause to become amicable, to settle or resolve*

Reconcile relationships even those that you say are hard to reconcile.

Forgive past hurts and mistakes. We cannot change the past. We can decide where we want to go in the future and give ourselves the best chance of getting there. We must aim high to make life a winning life!

Forgive those who have hurt you; do not dwell on the past. Forgive people, including family members, become reconciled.

The Bible, *Matthew 6:15* says, *But if you do not forgive men their sins, your Father will not forgive your sins.*

Forgive those who are hard to forgive. As I said before, you don't have to break bread with them. God merely asks us to forgive them. We must leave retribution to heaven.

Allow bygones to be bygones--forget past disagreements and past failures. Remember that there is no such thing as a failure. There are only outcomes. If your effort produced a result that was not your ideal outcome, then change what went wrong next time. Make a commitment to do better.

Build new relationships.

Develop rapport with people.

Don't envy people.

Reconcile even when people act as though they don't want to—do your part anyway. Conflicts are a natural part of life. Conflicts create friction and cause stress. But we must do our part to reconcile with people and behave according to *Ephesians 4:26, "Be ye angry, and sin not: let not the sun go down upon your wrath:"*

✝✝✝✝✝✝

✝

Lord, make me an instrument of your peace; where there is hatred, let me sow love; where there is injury, pardon; where there is doubt, faith; where there is despair, hope; where there is darkness, light; and where there is sadness, joy.

-Francis of Assisi

✝

Yes, GOD's Message: 'You're going to look at this place, these empty and desolate towns of Judah and streets of Jerusalem, and say, "A wasteland. Unlivable. Not even a dog could live here." But the time is coming when you're going to hear laughter and celebration, marriage festivities, people exclaiming, "Thank GOD-of-the-Angel-Armies. He's so good! His love never quits," as they bring thank offerings into GOD's Temple. I'll **restore** *everything that was lost in this land. I'll make everything as good as new.' I, GOD, say so.*

-Jeremiah 33:9-11 (The Message)

Principle #8

RESTORE—*bring back to a state of vigor*

Restore your thoughts! Bring yourself back to a state of vigor.

Have more childlike tendencies…. ignore those people who say "grow up and stop acting like a child."

Michael Jackson and Stevie Wonder both sang a song titled *With a Child's Heart* –

Find the lyrics and then play the song and sing along; if you don't have the song in your music collection, visit YouTube.com. Get the lyrics deep into your subconscious and **restore** yourself back to a state of vigor.

Create a reminder to keep in your purse or wallet or vehicle, keep it visible at work and read the words when you need motivation.

I believe the words will **restore** you back to a childlike appreciation for life.

I believe when de-motivated and in need of inspiration, if you sing the song *With a Child's Heart* you will *stay motivated* throughout the day. And, no matter what comes your way you will not allow it to ever get you down. Always believe in your heart and give thanks that our Creator, God is in charge of the day. *Cast all your cares upon Him for He cares for you. I Peter 5:7*

✞✞✞✞✞✞

✠

Resolve *never to quit, never to give up,*
no matter what the situation.

~Jack Nicklaus

"There is nothing that any human being *knows*, or *can do*, that they have not learned."

Principle #9

RESOLVE—*decide firmly on a course of action*

Resolve to keep learning. **Resolve** to keep growing. **Resolve** not to be poor. **Resolve** to make a difference in the world.

Resolve to never give up on your dreams and goals.

Founder of Mary Kay, Mary Kay Ash's husband died the month before the new business venture was supposed to start.

Kentucky Fried Chicken, KFC's Founder Colonel Sanders was at retirement age when his chicken recipe became famous.

One of the top clinics in our country, the Mayo Clinic was founded by Dr. William Worrall at the age of 70.

Astronaut John Glenn returned to space at the age of 77.

Michael Jordan was cut from his high school basketball team because he was told he was not ready for varsity basketball.

Thomas Edison's teachers said he was too stupid to learn anything. He was fired from his first two jobs for being nonproductive.

The humorous war novel, M*A*S*H, by Richard Hooker was rejected by 21 publishers.

These people were ordinary regular folks like us. They resolved to never quit. You see, a *winner never quits and a quitter never wins*.

Resolve not to live in either the past or the future. **Resolve** to always concentrate on the present. Simply meaning that we should concentrate on our activity or goal at that time. If we are running, concentrate on running and when you look up, you will have finished the race because you concentrated on running.

At the beginning of the New Year many people make resolutions to be different. We resolve to lose weight and change our eating habits. We make a resolution that we will exercise more or even just get started on an exercise program.

The Bible is the most widely read book and one goal that people often set is to read the Bible more or try and read the Bible in one year.

People make a resolution to save more money and pay off debts. We **resolve** not to be poor. After all, "the earth is the Lord's and the fullness thereof, the world and they that dwell therein." "The Lord is our shepherd we shall not want."

Can you agree that hurricanes and tornadoes do a lot of damage. But, termites do more damage than both hurricanes and tornadoes. Like the termite we must **resolve** to chip away daily to accomplish our dreams and goals.

Everything we know we had to learn it. In infancy we started learning. **Resolve** to engage in lifelong learning.

Learning to crawl and walk, to put on our clothes, reading a book, solving a math problem, attaining skills for a job, computing, spelling a word, the art of golfing, swimming, riding a bike, or driving a car, running a successful business, there is nothing that any human being *knows* or *can do* that they have not learned.

It's possible to get a lot more done and accomplished every day if we **resolve** to work at a task like it is the day before vacation. Most people seem to accomplish more tasks on the day before they go on vacation. They seem to have a lot more determination and energy to get things done on that day. They **resolve** to just get it done!

We start each year off with a bang. Achieving lifelong goals is not an overnight hobby or quick fix. It takes a strong willed person to take action on an inspired goal.

Let's *Always Stay Motivated* and make our resolutions stick. Have fun doing so!

✞✞✞✞✞✞

✝

Determination gives the **resolve** *to keep going in spite of roadblocks that lay before you.*

~Denis Waitley

Della Faye's
Favorite Quotations
and Scriptures to
Always Stay Motivated

✝

Wallowing in self-pity leads to nothingness.
Self-discipline leads to accomplishments.

-Della Faye

✝

"Blessed is the man who walks not in the counsel of the ungodly, nor stands in the path of sinners, nor sits in the seat of the scornful;

But his delight is in the law of the Lord, and in His law he meditates day and night.

He shall be like a tree planted by the rivers of water that brings forth its fruit in its season, whose leaf also shall not wither, and whatever he does shall prosper."

-Psalm 1:1-3

✠

"Into each life some rain must fall.
When it rains
look for the rainbow."

-Anonymous

****

✠

"If you want the rainbow,
you've got to put up with
a little rain."

-Dolly Parton

✟

*"The whole world
steps aside for the man
who knows where
he is going."*

-Anonymous

✝

"What would you
attempt to do
if you knew you
could not fail?"

-Anonymous

✟

*"You can kill
a man but
you can't
kill an idea."*

-Medgar Evers

✟

*"We aim above the mark
to hit the mark."*

-Ralph Waldo Emerson

✝

*"A good goal is like a
strenuous exercise —
it makes you stretch."*

-Mary Kay Ash

✝

*"Our doubts are
traitors, and make us
lose the good we oft
might win by fearing
to attempt."*

-William Shakespeare

✝

"The future belongs to those who believe in the beauty of their dreams."

-Eleanor Roosevelt

✝

*"All men who have
achieved great things
have been great
dreamers."*

-Orison Swett Marden

✠

"A person has to have goals:
for a day and for a lifetime."

-Ted Williams

✠

"Great minds have purposes;
others have wishes."

-Washington Irving

✝

"Concentration is the key to economic results. No other principles of effectiveness is violated as constantly today as the basic principle of concentration."

-Peter Drucker

✝

*"The ability to
focus on one thing
single-mindedly and
see it through
until it's done
is critical to success."*

-Harvey Mackay

✞

"Spend more time preparing and less time regretting."

-Virginia Wade

✟

"For the earth
is the Lord's
and the fullness thereof;
the world, and they
that dwell therein.

-Psalms 24:1

✝

"When I hear
somebody sigh,
'life is hard,'
I am always
tempted to ask,
compared to what?"

-Sydney Harris

✝

*"You are never given
a wish without also
being given the power
to make it come true.
You may have to work
for it, however."*

-Richard Bach

✝

*"Faith ought not to be
a play thing. If we
believe, we should
believe like giants."*

-Mary McLeod Bethune

✝

*"Man is what
he believes."*

-Anton Chekhov

✝

*"If you keep on saying
things are going to be
bad, you have a good
chance of becoming a
prophet."*

-Isaac Bashevis Singer

✠

"All that we are
is the result
of what we have thought. . .
what we think we become."

-Buddha

✝

*"Since it doesn't
cost a dime to dream,
you'll never short-
change yourself when
you stretch your
imagination."*

-Robert Schuller

✞

*"Life reflects
your own thoughts
back to you."*

-Napoleon Hill

✞

*"Where do you
find motivation?
You find it
within yourself."*

-Michael Jordan

✝

"Everything is in the mind.
Knowing what you want
is the first step in getting it."

-Mae West

✝

*"If you can dream it
you can do it."*

-Walt Disney

✝

*"Everything that is
done in the world is
done by hope."*

-Martin Luther

✝

"Be hopeful!
For tomorrow
has never happened before."

-Robert Schuller

✝

"I am happy
and content
because I think I am."

-Alain

✝

"Follow your bliss.
Find where it is
and don't be afraid
to follow it."

-Joseph Campbell

✝

"It's a very short trip.
While alive, live."

-Malcolm Forbes

✟

"Whether you believe
you can do a thing
or not, you are right."

-Henry Ford

✝

"Efforts and courage
are not enough
without purpose
and direction."

-John F. Kennedy

✟

"The opera isn't over till the fat lady sings."

-Dan Cook

✝

". . . if thou canst believe,
all things are
possible to him
that believeth."

-Mark 9:23 (KJV)

✞

"Think BIG.
Act BIG.
Dream BIG."

-Conrad Hilton

✞

"Optimism is the
faith that leads
to achievement.
Nothing can be
done without
hope and confidence."

-Helen Keller

✝

*"We find in life
exactly what we put in."*

-Ralph Waldo Emerson

✞

"What is the recipe
for successful achievement?
Choose a career you love.
Give it the best there is in you.
Seize your opportunities.
And be a member of the team."

-Ben Franklin

✝

"If you chase two rabbits,
both will escape."

-Anonymous

✝

"Life is a journey. . .
every experience is here to teach
you more fully how to be
who you really are."

-Oprah Winfrey

✝

*"The way to get things done
is not to mind who gets the credit
for doing them."*

-Benjamin Jowett

✝

*"You get the best out of others
when you give the best of yourself."*

-Harry Firestone

✝

*"Outstanding leaders
go out of their way
to boost the self-esteem
of their personnel.
If people believe in themselves,
it's amazing what they can accomplish."*

-Sam Walton

✟

*"Put your information across slowly
and repeat it over and over again!
Take a difficult point
and make it so simple
that it will become clear
even to the dullard."*

-Knute Rockne

✝

"Motivation is everything.
You can do the work of two people,
but you can't be two people.
Instead, you have to inspire
the next guy down the line
and get him to inspire his people."

-Lee Iacocca

✝

"Thank God
For this
Abundance.
(TGFTA)."

-Anonymous

✢

"Write the bad things
that happen to you in the sand,
but write the good things
that happen to you
on a piece of marble."

-Arabic Parable

✝

"Problems are only opportunities in work clothes."

-Henry Kaiser

✝

"God grant me the serenity
to accept the things
I cannot change,
the courage
to change the things I can,
and the wisdom to
know the difference."

-Reinhold Niebuhr

✝

*"Ask the God
who made you
to keep
remaking you.*

-Norman Vincent Peale

✝

*"God allows us
to experience
the low points of life
in order to teach us lessons
that we could learn in
no other way."*

-C.S. Lewis

✝

*"Often God
shuts a door
in our face
so that he
can open the door
through which
he wants us to go."*

-Catherine Marshall

✝

*"Although the world
is full of suffering,
it is also full
of overcoming it."*

-Helen Keller

✝

*"The size of
your burden
is never as
important as the
way you carry it."*

-Lena Horne

✝

*"Have courage for the great sorrows
of life and patience for the small ones;
and when you have laboriously
accomplished your daily task,
go to sleep in peace.
God is awake."*

-Victor Hugo

✝

*"If God
simply handed us
everything we want,
he'd be taking from us
our greatest prize—
the joy of accomplishment."*

-Frank A. Clark

✝

*"I now have
an abundance of money
that supplies all my
financial needs,
financial wants, and
financial desires."*

-Anonymous

✝

*"Never confuse a single mistake
with a final mistake."*

-F. Scott Fitzgerald

✝

*"To be successful
you have got to
be willing to fail."*

-William Saroyan

✝

"God gives talent.
Work transforms talent
into genius."

-Anna Pavlova

✝

*"The great virtue of man
lies in his ability
to correct his mistakes
and continually make a
new man of himself."*

-Wang Yang-ming

✝

"Don't resist the way things are,
instead put your energies
into transforming them
or transforming yourself."

-Anonymous

✝

*"Our greatest weakness
lies in giving up.
The most certain way to succeed
is to always try—just one more time."*

-Thomas Edison

✝

"But they that wait upon the Lord
shall renew their strength;
they shall mount up with wings as eagles;
they shall run, and not be weary;
and they shall walk, and not faint."

-Isaiah 40:31

About the Author

Della Faye is a keynote speaker, performance improvement trainer, business consultant, entrepreneur, community volunteer, and author. Her first book titled *Always Try Just One More Time*: was released in July 2005.

✝ ✝ ✝ ✝

Booking Information: Speaker, workshop leader, corporate trainer, women's retreats, youth programs, or program emcee:

www.dellafaye.com

Facebook
https://www.facebook.com/della.faye

Twitter
https://twitter.com/Della_Faye

YouTube.com under the name Della Faye

LinkedIn.com
www.linkedin.com/in/dellafaye